30p

SOMERSET
COUNTY LIBRARY
CANCELLED

# GREAT MYSTERIES
# SEA MYSTERIES

The sea has always played an important part in stories about mysterious events. There are tales about ships vanishing or being found without any of their crew aboard; about sailors seeing, or even being attacked by, monsters of all shapes and sizes; and about the 'Bermuda Triangle', where planes as well as ships disappear. Some of these cannot be true, but others . . . As you read this book, try to decide which events have happened and which are just sailors' stories.

# GREAT MYSTERIES
# SEA MYSTERIES

Ben Wilson

Illustrated by Tony Gibbons
and Martin Kingstone

# Great Mysteries

**Ancient Mysteries**
**Ghosts**
**Lands of Legend**
**Lost Treasures**
**Monster Mysteries**
**Sea Mysteries**
**The Supernatural**
**UFOs**

**Editor:** Stephen Setford
**Designer:** David Armitage
**Cover Illustration:** A sea serpent attacks some whalers who have tried to capture it.
**Frontispiece:** One of the most famous sea mysteries concerns the *Marie Celeste*, which was discovered drifting in the Atlantic Ocean on 3 December 1872 without any of her crew. The ship that found her sent some sailors aboard, who could find no clues to explain why the *Marie Celeste* had been abandoned.

First published in 1988 by
Wayland (Publishers) Limited
61 Western Road, Hove
East Sussex BN3 1JD, England

© Copyright 1988 Wayland (Publishers) Limited

British Library Cataloguing in Publication Data

Wilson, Ben
　Sea mysteries — (Great mysteries).
　1. Oceans. Mysteries
　I. Title II. Series
　001.9'4'09162

　ISBN 1-85210-355-8

Phototypeset by Oliver Dawkins Ltd, Burgess Hill, West Sussex
Printed in Italy by G. Canale & C.S.p.A, Turin
Bound in France by A.G.M.

# Contents

| | |
|---|---|
| The secrets of the sea | 6 |
| Vanished without trace! | 8 |
| The ships' graveyard | 10 |
| The Flying Dutchman – fact or fiction? | 14 |
| Ghosts and ghost ships | 16 |
| Crossing the Atlantic . . . in a boat made of reeds! | 20 |
| Who 'found' America? | 22 |
| A sea monster's deathly grip | 27 |
| Monsters of the deep | 28 |
| The quest for le Vasseur's treasure | 35 |
| Lost treasures | 36 |
| The sinking of the Lusitania | 40 |
| Conclusion | 42 |
| Glossary | 46 |
| Further reading | 47 |
| Index | 48 |

# The secrets of the sea

*A* coelacanth *from the Indian Ocean. This species of fish is over 60 million years old and was, until recently, thought to be extinct.*

*A diver exploring a wrecked ship off the Philippines, in the Pacific Ocean.*

The sea is the last great mystery which faces us here on earth. For even as we take our first hesitant footsteps into outer space, much of the underwater world, which makes up over 60 per cent of the earth's surface, remains unexplored and unknown to us. Humankind has mapped out the world's ocean surfaces, sailed the seven seas and built submarines to travel beneath the waves. But our knowledge of the geography of the ocean bed and of the countless varieties of creatures which inhabit this world below the waves is still relatively limited.

The sea keeps its secrets well. Only recently it was discovered that the *coelacanth,* a bluefish dating from 60 million years ago and thought to be extinct, still thrives in the Indian Ocean. Do other sea creatures dating back to pre-historic times still roam the ocean depths? Could some of the reported sightings of gigantic sea monsters actually be true?

Perhaps the sea also hides clues to our own past. Legends tell of a beautiful, fertile island, called Atlantis, which seems to have flourished some time between 10,000-1500 BC. The island was rich in minerals and vegetation and its people were extremely advanced in the sciences and the arts. However, it appears that Atlantis was completely destroyed in the space of 24 hours by a volcanic explosion and sunk beneath a tidal wave.

Did Atlantis really exist? Do its ruins lie somewhere on the ocean bed? There have been many claims for and against the existence of the city of Atlantis. Some people have claimed that the legend of Atlantis really refers to the ancient Minoan civilization which was based around the island of Crete, in the Mediterranean Sea. Others still insist that the ruins of this once-great civilization lie beneath the waters of the Atlantic Ocean. Edgar Cayce, a so-called 'visionary', claimed that Atlantis was destroyed in the year 10,000 BC by a huge explosion and that its true location was near a small island in the Bahamas called Bimini. Some years later, a number of stone structures were found off the coast of Bimini, but experts are divided about whether they are natural rock formations or the remains of walls of an ancient civilization.

The sea jealously guards a wealth of fascinating secrets. There are strange tales of the puzzling disappearance of ships and people in certain sea areas, of ghosts and ghost ships coming back to haunt or curse the living, of seemingly impossible sea voyages made long ago, and of treasures lost in the mists of time. These are the mysteries we will now set out to explore.

*The legendary city of Atlantis probably looked like this before it was destroyed by a large wave or an explosion.*

### Vanished without trace!

It is 4 March 1918. The First World War still rages on land and at sea. In the waters of the western North Atlantic, a 19,000-tonne supply vessel, called the USS *Cyclops,* leaves Barbados and sets sail for the American port of Norfolk, Virginia.

In command of the *Cyclops* is German-born Captain Worley, a man well known for his strange behaviour. On leaving Barbados, he inexplicably orders the ship to turn suddenly to the south, away from the planned route.

Then, without warning, all contact with the *Cyclops* is lost. An air and sea search finds no trace of the *Cyclops*, nor is there sign of any wreckage. It seems that no German submarines or mines were in the area at the time of the ship's disappearance.

What happened to the *Cyclops*? Was it struck by a freak wave or blown up by bombs planted by German spies? Was it betrayed by its odd captain? An official US Navy investigation rejects these explanations, calling the incident 'one of the most baffling mysteries in the history of the Navy.'

One fascinating theory remains: that the *Cyclops* became yet another victim of the mysterious region through which it travelled . . . the so-called Bermuda Triangle.

# The ships' graveyard

The area in which the USS *Cyclops* disappeared has been called the 'sea of lost ships' or 'the ships' graveyard'. Its actual name is the Sargasso Sea and it lies in the western region of the North Atlantic. Its most striking feature is the masses of seaweed which float on its surface. Sailors' legends tell of how ships became held forever in this web of weeds or were sucked beneath the surface in its deathly grip. Whatever the truth of these tales, there have been a series of baffling losses of ships in this region since records were started in 1800.

At the beginning of the nineteenth century, no less than three ships were mysteriously lost in this region in the space of 25 years. On 20 August 1800, the USS *Pickering* and her crew of 90 disappeared while heading for Guadeloupe, a group of islands in the Caribbean. Fourteen years later, the

*Crewmen from the* Ellen Austen *set out to investigate a schooner which was found abandoned near the Azores in 1881.*

### The 'Philadelphia Experiment'

Could an experiment, said to have been carried out in 1943, provide a clue to the secret of the Bermuda Triangle? It was designed to test the effects of a strong magnetic field on a manned ship. The results were amazing. At first, a hazy green light surrounded the vessel. Then, both ship and crew began to disappear! Soon, all trace of them had gone! Only after the magnetic field was switched off did they become visible again! It is even said that, for some months afterwards, members of the crew were prone to vanish and then re-appear! Are magnetic forces the key to the Triangle's mystery?

USS *Wasp* vanished without trace with 140 men lost. Then, in 1824, the USS *Wildcat* and her crew of 14 went missing shortly after setting sail from Cuba.

Ships have also been found adrift, abandoned by their crew for no apparent reason. In 1881, the *Ellen Austen* was passing west of the Azores when her crew came across an

*In 1945, five planes, like these, mysteriously vanished over what was later to be called the 'Bermuda Triangle'.*

abandoned schooner. Three men were placed aboard the schooner, but soon afterwards a storm blew up and she became separated from the *Ellen Austen*. When she was sighted two days later, the three crewmen had also disappeared! A second crew of three went aboard the schooner. Once again, a sudden storm separated the two ships. This time, however, they were never to meet again. The schooner and her crew had vanished, leaving behind a mystery which remains unsolved to this day.

It was in 1945, after five planes vanished while on a routine training flight, that this strange region began to attract worldwide interest. Shortly before contact with the planes was lost, the pilots reported that their instruments were 'going crazy', that they had lost their bearings and that they were 'entering white water'. Because their flight path had followed a triangular route, whose apex was in direct line with the island of Bermuda, the region became known as the 'Bermuda Triangle'.

Even with the aid of modern technology, no one can explain the strange power of the Bermuda Triangle to swallow up ships and aircraft. But what is it like to experience this frightening and unknown force? Captain Don Henry was in charge of a tug which was towing an empty barge to Fort Lauderdale, USA, in 1966. The sea was calm and weather conditions were good. Without warning, the tug's compass began to spin wildly. Then, in Henry's words, 'the horizon disappeared — the water, sky and horizon all blended together. We couldn't see where we were'. The barge was covered in a milky-coloured cloud, while the sea around it became choppy and disturbed. At that moment, the tug's electrical power failed. It was slowly being pulled back into the cloud. Henry pushed the tug's throttle full ahead and, after a long struggle, managed to pull the barge clear. Later, he said that it had felt like 'being pulled in two directions at the same time'.

What theories have been offered to explain the mystery of the Bermuda Triangle? It has been suggested that violent underwater currents may suck ships to their doom in seconds or cause huge tidal waves to overwhelm them. Some have even claimed it is UFOs which hijack the ships and kidnap their crews in order to examine them? Do the remains of an ancient civilization which had advanced powers lie within the Triangle? Does it still send out pulses of

---

**Other mysterious disappearances**

**1880** HMS *Atlanta* and her crew of 290 cadets disappear without trace.

**1902** A German ship, the *Freya*, is discovered adrift with no crew on board. They are never found.

**1932** The *John and Mary* is found abandoned in perfect weather conditions only 80 km from Bermuda.

**1963** A huge freighter, the *Marine Sulphur Queen*, disappears.

**1973** The *Anita*, a 20,000-tonne freighter, is lost together with her crew of 32.

*In 1966, Captain Don Henry's tug,* Good News, *was almost sucked into a mysterious milky-coloured cloud while sailing through the Bermuda Triangle.*

energy which cause havoc to the surrounding seas and skies? Or is the true explanation that the area is subject to strange magnetic forces which can cause planes and boats to vanish and be whisked to another time and place?

Perhaps these ideas are merely the product of people's imaginations, and there is a simple, more logical explanation to these disappearances which has been overlooked or ignored.

### The Flying Dutchman — fact or fiction?

In the early seventeenth century, Captain Hendrik van der Decken sets sail from Amsterdam aboard the *Flying Dutchman*. He is bound for the East Indies. A greedy and foolish man, he is determined to make his fortune on this trip.

All goes well until the ship begins to round the dangerous waters of the Cape of Good Hope. For days fierce storms batter the ship. In spite of the pleas of the passengers and the crew to seek sheltered waters, Captain van der Decken heartlessly pursues his course. He drinks and smokes, pausing only to fill the air with curses.

Suddenly, a strange form appears on deck. It announces that it is the Devil and challenges van der Decken to oppose God's will by sailing into the teeth of the storm. The Dutch captain agrees . . . and brings down God's curse on his head:

> 'You are condemned to sail on until the Day of Judgement, without rest and without ever making land.'

From that day onwards, the *Flying Dutchman* is doomed to roam the seas, bringing ill fortune and disaster on any vessel which might cross her path. The tale of the ghost ship might seem to be the stuff of legend. But there are numerous accounts of those people who claim to have seen her . . . and suffered as a result!

# Ghosts and ghost ships

The sea has been a place of danger and death for many sailors. As a result, a number of superstitions and legends have arisen about those lost at sea and the ships they sailed in. Most of these, of course, are the work of many a sailor's vivid imagination told and re-told with ever more fantastic details added. But there remains a handful of genuinely puzzling ghostly sea mysteries which still send a tingle of fear down the spine.

Mystery surrounds the tale of the *Ourang Medan*, a Dutch freighter which was bound for Jakarta, Indonesia, in February 1948. On a day of calm seas and clear blue skies, she sent out the following SOS call which was picked up by over a dozen ships:

'Captain and all officers dead. Entire crew dead or dying. Now I am also near death'.

A grim sight awaited the rescue team which reached the stricken vessel three hours later. The deck was littered with

*Was it a horrific monster that terrified the crew of the* Ourang Medan *to death in 1948? We will never know.*

corpses, while on the bridge lay the dead bodies of the officers and the captain. Each man appeared to have died in the same way, eyes fixed in horror and arms raised to the sky. Even the ship's dog lay with its fangs bared and its paws arched in the air, as if trying to ward off an invisible enemy. The rescue team's doctor could find no trace of poisoning, disease or of any fumes that might have caused the deaths. What was the cause? The question has never been answered satisfactorily.

Why should a photograph of two men swimming in the Pacific be one of the most remarkable ever taken? Because the two men, James Courtenay and Michael Meehan, had been killed four days before the photograph was taken! They had been overcome by poisonous fumes while working in the engine room of the oil tanker, *Waterton*. On 3 December 1929, the day after they had been buried at sea, an astonished deckhand spotted the two men swimming just 15 metres from the tanker. Over the course of the next three days, the men were to appear frequently, smiling and waving at their astonished crewmates. On the tanker's next voyage, a member of the crew managed to take eight photographs of Courtenay and Meehan. Unfortunately, only one of the photos gave a clear picture. But, it was enough. Friends and relatives of the two men had no doubt that the two swimmers were Courtenay and Meehan!

Perhaps the most well-known sea mystery is that of the *Marie Celeste*, the 'ghost ship' found adrift off the Azores on 3 December 1872. There was no sign of life on board, either above or below decks. There were no clues to explain why the crew had disappeared. Indeed everything appeared to be quite normal. In the crew's quarters, clothing lay folded neatly on bunks and washing hung on lines. In the galley,

*One of the photographs taken of Courtenay and Meehan, swimming next to the tanker* Waterton, *after they had been killed by poisonous fumes in the ship's engine room.*

### The ghost ship of the Goodwins

The *Lady Lovibond* ran aground on the Goodwin Sands, off south-east England, on 13 February 1748. At the time a wedding celebration was being held on board. Fifty years later to the day, a three-masted schooner identical to the *Lady Lovibond* was seen heading towards the Goodwins. Voices and laughing could be heard, followed by screams of terror as she ran aground. On both 13 February 1848 and 1898, the same ghostly sight was seen, and the same sounds of joy followed by horror. In 1948, many people watched for her, but nothing was seen. Will she return in 1998?

*What made the captain of the Marie Celeste abandon his ship, along with his crew, halfway through his breakfast?*

breakfast had been prepared and some of it had been served. In the captain's cabin, breakfast had been left. Next to it, the captain's log showed entries up to 25 November and gave no hint of anything being wrong.

Why was the *Marie Celeste* abandoned? It seems unlikely that bad weather was the cause. There was little sign of damage on deck and the ship had taken in only a normal amount of water. Was there a mutiny? There was no sign of a struggle and, in any case, why would the mutineers have left the ship too?

Instead of answers, there remains one final question. How did the *Marie Celeste* remain on her intended course for ten days and some 800 km with no one at the wheel to steer her? Stories grew up that the ship was cursed. Although she was recovered and put to sea again, she had an unhappy history. She was sold 17 times in 11 years before being run aground deliberately off the coast of Haiti in 1884, taking her terrible secret to a watery grave.

## The ghost of the UB65

The Second Officer of the German UB65 submarine was killed when one of her own torpedoes accidently exploded in her hold. For months after the accident, the Second Officer was seen by members of the crew in different parts of the submarine. One crewman was driven mad by the ghost's presence and threw himself overboard to his doom. Even a pastor could not rid the submarine of her unwanted visitor. Finally, on 10 July 1918, just as the UB65 was about to be attacked by an American submarine, the German vessel was ripped apart by a terrible explosion from within. Could the ghost of the UB65 have taken its terrible and final revenge?

### Crossing the Atlantic . . . in a boat made of reeds!

As the coast of Central America comes within view, Thor Heyerdahl, the Norwegian adventurer and scientist, has good reason to feel happy. Many people have ridiculed his claim that the ancient Egyptians could have made the perilous journey across the Atlantic over 2,500 years ago in boats made of papyrus reeds. But now he has proved it was possible by completing the voyage from Morocco to Central America in a reed boat.

Heyerdahl used detailed drawings made by the artists of the ancient Egyptian Pharaohs. These showed every stage of the making of the reed boats, from the way the reeds were cut, bundled and lashed together, to the design of the steering gear and the layout of the rigging.

Heyerdahl's first attempt to make the crossing was in 1969, in *Ra I*. The journey was full of difficulties owing to the raft becoming waterlogged in rough weather. Finally, the eight-man crew had been forced to abandon their 17-metre craft when it was struck by a freak wave only a short distance from its goal.

However, just two years later, *Ra II* has successfully completed the voyage with relatively little trouble. Heyerdahl has proved that ancient civilizations could have made contact with one another, thanks to the slender papyrus reed and the skill of the Egyptians.

# Who 'found' America?

*A painting of Christopher Columbus, the famous explorer. He lived from 1451 to 1506. The native Americans (or 'Indians') were, of course, the first people to discover America. But was Columbus the first European to sail there?*

Most of us are familiar with the story of Christopher Columbus's historic voyage from Spain to the shores of America in 1492. He bravely defied dire warnings that, by setting a continuous course to the west across the Atlantic, he and his ships would fall off the edge of the world or be consumed by savage sea monsters. Instead of meeting such a fate, he actually opened up the route to the 'New World', America, although he thought at first that it was the East Indies. Columbus is therefore looked upon as the person who 'discovered' the vast continent of America. But is this claim actually true? There is evidence that other people visited this 'New World' long before Columbus.

Some archaeologists believe that the earliest sea voyages to the American continent were made by the Chinese and Japanese, crossing the Pacific as long ago as 3000 BC. They have uncovered Japanese-style pottery of that period in the coastal regions of Ecuador. Several sculptures, seemingly of Buddhist idols, have also been unearthed in South America and have been dated at around 2000 BC.

*A sixteenth-century painting showing Columbus arriving in North America. Was he the first European or had other people beaten him to it?*

*One person who may have reached North America before Columbus was Saint Brendan. He and 14 other monks crossed the Atlantic Ocean in AD 540 in a boat like this one.*

Similarly, could ancient Mediterranean peoples, such as the skilled sea-going Phoenicians and Carthaginians, have successfully made the perilous journey across the Atlantic? The philosophers Plato and Aristotle both wrote of a marvellous and mysterious overseas land first visited by the Phoenicians in 1000 BC and kept a closely-guarded secret for trade purposes. Other legends describe thrilling voyages across a vast ocean beyond the Pillars of Hercules (Gibraltar) to lands of great riches. One of these, dating from 500 BC, describes a voyage through slow-moving waters which sound similar to those of the Sargasso Sea:

> 'No breeze drives the ships, so dead is the wind of this sluggish sea . . . there is much seaweed among the waves it holds back the ships.'

Perhaps the strangest claim concerns Saint Brendan, an Irish monk who is said to have set sail for the 'land promised to the saints' in a 12-metre wooden boat covered with oxhide

*The Vikings, it is thought, crossed the treacherous Atlantic Ocean from Europe to North America in ships like these.*

in the year AD 540. Details of the voyage are recorded in a tenth-century Latin manuscript. This tells of how Brendan and his 14 colleagues set sail from Ireland on a northerly course and passed 'floating towers of crystal', sailed through thick fogs, came across strange sea creatures and landed on two small islands before reaching their promised land. Was this land America?

Although many of the details contained in the story seem incredible, it is thought that Brendan did actually make such a voyage. Some experts believe that his route took him to Greenland, the Newfoundland Banks and the small island of Labrador. He then skirted the coast of North America, stopped off at an island in the Bahamas and ended up in the area we now know as Florida.

We may never know for sure whether Brendan's epic travels really took him across the Atlantic, but it does now seem certain that another legendary sea journey was based on fact. The Norse sagas, written in the mid-fourteenth century, tell of the dramatic adventures of the heroic Viking leader, Leif Ericson. Around the year AD 1000 he led a convoy of Norse ships on a spectacular journey that took in Iceland, Greenland and, finally, North America. The description of the geography, climate and wildlife of the new land contained in the Norse sagas match those of Newfoundland. Recently a stone village dating back to Viking times has been discovered in northern Newfoundland. Could this village be the physical proof that Leif Ericson led the Vikings to America?

The question of who really did first sail the seas to 'discover' America may never be answered with certainty. Columbus may have 'sailed the ocean blue in 1492' to set foot in the 'New World', but perhaps he was only following in the wake of a string of skilful navigators and valiant explorers who had made the journey before him?

*A statue of Leif Ericson. According to the Norse sagas, he led some Viking ships across the Atlantic in AD 1000. They arrived in North America after visiting Iceland, Greenland and Newfoundland.*

### A sea monster's deathly grip

The year is 1942. Lieutenant Cox's thirst grows worse under the fierce sun. For three days, he and 11 other British sailors have been adrift in a flimsy liferaft in the remote and dangerous waters of the South Atlantic.

With horror, Cox sees a threatening dark shape in the water alongside the raft. It is at least 8 metres in length and has a broad head.

'Am I imagining things?' Cox wonders as he makes out two large eyes staring at him from beneath the waves.

Then, slowly and deliberately, a number of enormous tentacles emerge from the water. They reach out and coil around a man at the rear of the raft. Cox and the other men struggle to prise him free from the vice-like grip of the tentacles. But all their efforts are in vain. The poor victim is lifted from the raft like a baby from a cradle. He disappears, wrapped in the monster's arms.

Cox and his men, wounded in the life and death struggle, prepare for another attack. The creature clearly has the power to crush the liferaft and devour all on board. But, incredibly, it does not return. Cox, along with only two other naval officers who survive, will live to tell this frightening tale.

What kind of creature was it that attacked the liferaft on that fateful day in 1942?

# Monsters of the deep

From the earliest times there have been stories and legends of strange and frightening sea monsters capable of bringing death and destruction to those who dared to venture into certain remote and unmapped areas of the oceans. Norse legend named one of these creatures the 'Kraken', a type of squid or octopus so huge that it could overturn fishing boats, whaling vessels and even ships. This frightening creature had thick, long tentacles with huge sucker pads and rows of claws to grip its prey, while its 'mouth' was a beak which was capable of cutting through wire and of piercing the side of a ship.

Could it have been a Kraken which attacked a fishing boat off Newfoundland in 1873? The two fishermen on board had prodded what appeared to be a large mass of seaweed heading for their boat and were horrified when it reared up

*A painting of a huge, octopus-like Kraken attacking a merchant ship in the late eighteenth century.*

in the water and seized their vessel in two huge tentacles. It looked like a large squid or octopus. Repeated blows with an axe eventually forced the wounded monster to release its deadly hold on the boat, leaving behind a piece of tentacle 6 metres long. Experts calculated that it belonged to a creature 20 metres in length.

John Starkey reports a chilling encounter with a Kraken-like creature that came alongside his naval patrol-ship in the Indian Ocean one evening in 1942. He recalls 'two cold green eyes' staring up from the water, tentacles half a metre thick and describes the creature as being longer than the ship — at least 50 metres in length! Fortunately, the monster made no attack.

Other ships have not been so lucky. In 1872, the crew of the steamer *Strathowen* claimed they saw 'a giant squid' topple a 150-tonne schooner, the *Pearl*, and drag it beneath the waves. In the 1930s, a 15,000-tonne tanker called the *Brunswick* claimed to have survived three attacks by Kraken-like monsters.

*Another monster of the deep is the giant sea serpent. One is said to have been spotted by the crew of HMS* Daedalus *while they were rounding the Cape of Good Hope in 1848.*

There have been many reported sightings of another legendary monster of the deep, the sea serpent. The most famous of these occurred in 1848, when sailors aboard HMS *Daedalus*, a 19-tonne frigate, spotted a strange creature while rounding the Cape of Good Hope. Captain Peter McQuhae later confirmed that it was a sea serpent, 20 metres in length, which swam alongside the *Daedalus* for over 20 minutes. The body was dark brown. Its head was raised about a metre out of the water, revealing jaws large enough to hold a fully-grown man and lined with fierce jagged teeth.

In 1852, the whaling ships the *Monongahela* and the *Rebecca Sims* were scouring the Pacific when a whale was sighted. Three longboats were lowered from the *Monongahela* in pursuit of the creature, which proved to be huge — some 45 metres in length. Stuck with harpoons, the creature's wild threshing smashed two longboats, but after a fierce struggle, it was hauled alongside the ship. Too long to take on board, only the remarkable head with its cruel teeth was cut off and preserved in a pickling vat. The *Monongahela* never reached home. Ship and crew disappeared. Wreckage was found off the coast of Alaska some weeks later. There was no explanation. Was the ship

**Opposite** *This map shows where sea monsters, of all shapes and sizes, have supposedly been sighted over the years.*

*A sea serpent, with a head like a turtle's, was said to have attacked a liferaft in 1962 and carried off four of its occupants.*

attacked and destroyed by another monster?

In 1962, a liferaft carrying five men was attacked by a sea serpent. Its head and neck resembled that of a turtle and stretched over 4 metres out of the water. Hissing horribly, it gave off a foul-smelling odour of rotting fish. After capsizing the raft, the monster carried off four of the men, leaving one survivor to recount the terrifying tale.

**Below** *A photograph of 'Morgawr', a monster reportedly seen off the coast of Cornwall, south-western Britain, in February 1976. It was about 8 metres long.*

### The *Architeuthis*

In 1857, the Kraken was given a Latin name by scientists, *Architeuthis*. The largest specimen ever measured was washed up on St. Augustine's Beach, Florida, in 1896. Its tentacles measured about 9 metres and its original length was estimated to have been 20 metres. Many sailors claim to have seen giant *Architeuthis* doing battle with sperm whales. One captured sperm whale had sucker scars measuring 36 cm on its body, suggesting that its foe measured around 150 metres – half the height of the Eiffel Tower in Paris!

**Above** *A sea serpent which, it is said, was seen frequently off the coast of Massachusetts, USA, in the 1800s.*

**Right** *A nineteenth-century picture making fun of people who said they had seen monsters at sea.*

*A sea monster photographed in Stonehaven Bay, Hook Island, Australia, on 12 December 1964.*

Some sea monsters choose to haunt waters closer to land. One such creature is supposed to roam the Strait of Georgia, between Vancouver Island and British Columbia, off the west coast of Canada. It was first sighted by native North Americans long before white settlers arrived, and is known as Cadborosaurus or 'Caddy'. In this century it has been seen by over 100 people and has been described as being a sea serpent 15 metres long, with huge, wide jaws.

In 1965, a Belgian zoologist, Dr Bernard Heuvelmans, began the most detailed study of sea serpents to date. He examined 587 sightings dating from 1639 to 1964 and concluded that 358 were genuine. From these, he divided the sea serpents into nine types. Could the oceans really be roamed by so many species of sea monster? If so, how many more are yet to be discovered?

**Monsters sighted around the world**

**1882** Llandudno, North Wales: 'a large, dark, undulating creature as big as a large steamer.'

**1893** Cape Town, South Africa: 'a giant eel, 25 metres long, with jaws 2 metres wide.'

**1964** Great Barrier Reef, Australia: 'a gigantic beast, 20 metres long, with jaws 1 metre wide.'

**1966** North Atlantic: 'a writhing, twisting monster, between 10 and 12 metres long.'

**1976** Cornwall, England: a monster, nicknamed 'Morgawr' (sea giant), measuring about 8 metres, is spotted and photographed.

## The quest for le Vasseur's treasure

The year is 1730. As the notorious French pirate, Olivier le Vasseur climbs the gallows and a noose is placed around his neck, he lays down a challenge, 'Find my treasure who can!' With these words he throws a chart to the spectators. The chart, and other papers of le Vasseur found later, contain strange diagrams and messages written in code. Who could unlock le Vasseur's secret?

For over 200 years the mystery remained unsolved. Then, in 1949, Reginald Cruise-Wilkins is shown some papers and a number of rocks on a beach at Bel Ombre in the Seychelles. Similar weird markings have been made on each of them. After studying the markings, Cruise-Wilkins feels sure they are the clues left by le Vasseur. He believes he can interpret them.

Following the directions in the papers, Cruise-Wilkins begins to dig at Bel Ombre. At several sites he finds buried statues and carvings. A pattern begins to emerge: each site stands for one of the 12 labours of the mythical Greek hero Hercules.

After 20 years of searching, Cruise-Wilkins reaches the site of the twelfth labour. It is a cave, marked by a carving of Cerberus, the three-headed dog who guarded the Underworld. Cruise-Wilkins is convinced that le Vasseur's treasure lies beneath it. Sadly, he died before he could dig it up.

# Lost treasures

How many treasures still lie in sunken wrecks at the bottom of the ocean waiting to be discovered? A great many it seems. Modern bounty hunters now use the very latest high-technology equipment to seek out underwater treasure troves. These scavengers of the sea-bed are modern pirates and there are rich pickings to be won.

But time and tide still defy even the efforts of these experts. The *Lutine* was wrecked off the coast of the Netherlands in 1799. Because of the dangerous storms and treacherous tides that occur in this region, her rich cargo of gold, silver and notes to the value of two million pounds is largely untouched. Over the years, the wreck has become covered in silt and sand so that its precise location is no longer known.

Similarly, a British vessel, the *Grosvenor*, foundered while rounding Cape Horn in 1873. Her cargo of gold and jewels would be worth over half a million pounds today. Yet all efforts to locate the wreck have failed and it seems doubtful that anyone will uncover her lost treasures.

*The* Lutine *foundering on rocks off the coast of the Netherlands in 1799. Her cargo of £2 million has never been recovered.*

Between the sixteenth and eighteenth centuries, the high seas were a place of great danger for ships carrying valuable cargoes. Pirates roamed the most frequently-used trade routes seeking out galleons bearing valuable cargoes. The most successful pirates would hide their ill-gotten gains in secret locations, often on remote islands. Popular legends quickly arose concerning these burial sites. One such legend is about Cocos Island, which lies in the Pacific, 560 km from the coast of Costa Rica.

It seems that treasure was brought to the island on at least three occasions. In the seventeenth century, an English pirate named Edward Davies landed seven boatloads of booty there. A few years later, over 6 million pounds' worth of various treasures was hidden on the island by another pirate, Bonito Benito. Then, in 1821, an English captain called Thomson seized a cargo of treasures that he was supposed to be transporting to Spain on board his ship, the *Mary Dear*. Once again, the dense forests of Cocos Island were chosen as the hiding place.

*The pirate Edward Davies landing on Cocos Island, in the Pacific Ocean, where he is meant to have buried seven boatloads of treasure.*

It seems that these treasures were never recovered by the pirates. As a result, a number of bounty hunters launched expeditions to try and find them. The most successful of these was a carpenter named John Keating, who recovered a huge fortune in gold in 1844. Auguste Gissler spent 17 years (1889-1906) searching for Benito's treasure, but he only uncovered 33 gold coins! An explorer named Peter Bergman claimed to have discovered Benito's hoard in a remote cave in 1929. He was unable to remove much of the gold and silver, however, and when he tried to find the cave a second time he found it impossible to retrace his route. So, much of Benito's treasure still remains untouched. The last great treasure hunt on Cocos Island took place in 1939. James Forbes, great grandson of a crew member of the *Mary Dear*, began digging at a previously unexplored site. But he was unsuccessful and left the island with nothing to show for his efforts.

Did the most notorious pirates of the eighteenth century leave behind great stores of treasure that are yet to be discovered? Blackbeard Teach was a cruel and ruthless pirate who preyed on treasure ships in the Caribbean. In 1717, he buried a huge iron chest containing valuable booty

*Blackbeard Teach watches two of his crewmen bury some of his treasure on the island of Plum. These men, along with four others from the crew, were later shot by Teach so that only he would know where the treasure lay.*

*Pirates attacking a merchant ship laden with a cargo of treasure.*

on a small island called Plum. To make sure that no one could reveal its location, Teach shot the six helpers he had taken along. It was not until 1928 that two local fishermen on the island discovered a freshly-dug hole with the imprint of a chest at the bottom. Had Teach's treasure been found?

In 1691, the wicked Captain William Kidd seized the precious cargo of the *Quedah Merchant*. Kidd buried gold bars and coins worth £14,000 (which was then a huge sum) at Gardiner's Island, New York. He was eventually caught and, during his trial, he revealed where he had buried some of his treasure. Despite this co-operation, he was still sentenced to death. On the day before he was due to be hung, Kidd offered to reveal the whereabouts of the rest of the *Quedah Merchant*'s treasure. His offer was refused because most people thought that little of the loot remained to be uncovered. But according to popular myth, Kidd's treasure is still waiting to be found.

### The sinking of the Lusitania

On 7 May 1915, during the First World War, the British luxury passenger liner, the *Lusitania*, is steaming at over 20 knots off the south coast of Ireland. She carries over a thousand passengers together with a cargo of food and brass rods. She is also transporting over 4,000 cases of ammunition to Britain.

Captain William Turner is nervous because he knows that German submarines are active off the south coast of Ireland. At 2.11 pm, the cry goes up, 'Torpedo! Torpedo on the starboard side!' Within seconds it strikes the *Lusitania* below the bridge. Just 18 minutes later, the ship lies at the bottom of the ocean and 1,198 people are dead.

The sinking of the *Lusitania* marks a turning-point in the First World War. For among those killed are 124 Americans, and their deaths help to bring the USA into the war against Germany. But mystery surrounds the incident even to this day. Were the *Lusitania* and her innocent passengers deliberately sacrificed to bring the United States into the War? Why was her escort of destroyers taken away, when it was known that U-boats lay in her path? Did the liner sink so quickly because she was carrying an even larger, secret cargo of ammunition, which exploded when struck by the torpedo?

British Admiralty records covering the disaster were mysteriously 'lost'. But the suspicion remains that the *Lusitania* was lured into a trap designed by the British.

# Conclusion

Ever since humans first looked out across the wide ocean and wondered what lay beyond the horizon, the sea has been a constant source of fascination and wonder for us. Ancient peoples imagined that the sea was a god, or the home of a number of gods, who controlled its various moods. Today, in the age of space travel and computers, few people believe such ideas. But the sea still remains outside our control. It holds mysteries we cannot yet explain. It possesses secrets we may never unlock.

*Mermaids, half-woman and half-fish, are said to live in the sea. Do they exist? They do — according to this nineteenth-century painting!*

**Left** *We have always been fascinated by the hidden world beneath the oceans' waves. Here is a 'diver' in the sixteenth century investigating underwater life.*

There may indeed be logical explanations to all the mysteries that have been discussed. The Bermuda Triangle contains some of the most heavily-used shipping routes in the world. The losses in the area may be so high only because a lot of ships pass through it. It may be that the strange stories of ghosts and ghost ships are caused by mirages, hallucinations or overworked imaginations. The sea monsters that have caused so much terror may have been harmless manatees (animals a bit like whales). Those 'monsters' which have claimed human victims may be no more than huge squid or whales.

**Below** *A mosaic (a picture made from coloured pieces of stone) of Proteus, one of the ancient Greeks' gods of the sea.*

It is possible that stories of voyages to the American continent before Columbus are just legends. Perhaps archaeological discoveries may one day either prove or disprove these theories. Likewise, research and investigation may eventually clear up the mystery surrounding the sinking of the *Lusitania*, and the tales of buried pirate treasure.

*An 8-metre-long squid was said to have been seen by* Alecton's *crew off the Canary Islands on 30 November 1861. True or false?*

But for the time being, you must make up your own mind. Is the sea the last great area of the unknown on earth, holding many secrets which await our discovery? Or are the mysteries of the sea no more than superstitions which have no place in the modern world? What do you think?

**Above** *Perhaps sea monsters are only angry whales?*

**Below** *One of the sea's secrets revealed: a part of the Titanic's deck.*

# Glossary

**Apex**  The tip or highest point of a triangle.

**Aristotle**  A famous Greek philosopher and writer (384-322 BC).

**Captain's log**  Record of a ship's voyage kept by the captain.

**Civilizations**  Highly-advanced peoples or races.

**Epic**  On a grand scale.

**Hallucinations**  Imagined experiences which appear to be real.

**High technology**  The most modern and efficient form of a particular piece of equipment.

**Foundered**  Filled with water and sank.

**Galleon**  A large Spanish trading ship.

**Magnetic**  Possessing an invisible force which attracts or repels certain objects.

**Minerals**  Substances in the earth which can be dug out and used (for example, coal, iron ore, gold and diamonds).

**Mirage**  Seeing something that does not exist.

**Mutiny**  A rebellion by a crew against its captain.

**Mythical**  Untrue.

**Norse**  Scandinavian.

**Pastor**  A priest.

**Plato**  A famous Greek philosopher and writer (428-348 BC).

**Salvager**  Someone who recovers sunken or wrecked vessels.

**Schooner**  A rigged vessel with two or more masts.

**Superstition**  Fear of the unknown.

**SOS**  Literally 'Save Our Souls'; the code sent out by a vessel in trouble.

**Undulating**  Moving up and down in gentle curves.

**UFOs**  Unidentified Flying Objects.

**U-Boats**  German submarines first used in the First World War (from the German *Untersee Boten*, meaning under-sea boats).

**Visionary**  Someone claiming to see the past or the future in his or her mind.

*Captain William Kidd, the seventeenth-century pirate. Where did he bury the treasure he seized from the Quedah Merchant?*

# Further Reading

If you would like to find out more about sea mysteries, you may like to read the following books:

Abranson, Eric, *Stories of the Sea* (Hodder & Stoughton, 1983)

Berlitz, Charles, *The Bermuda Triangle* (Souvenir, 1974)

Berlitz, Charles, *The Mystery of Atlantis* (Souvenir, 1970)

Blundell, Nigel, *The World's Greatest Mysteries* (Octopus, 1980)

Boar, Roger, and Blundell, Nigel, *The World's Greatest Ghosts* (Octopus, 1983)

Garrett, Richard, *Great Sea Mysteries* (Severn House Publishing, 1971)

Heyerdahl, Thor, *The Ra Expeditions* (Allen & Unwin, 1971)

Keel, John, *Strange Creatures from Time and Space* (Sphere, 1976)

Matthews, Rupert, *Monster Mysteries* (Wayland, 1988)

Pascal, Jeremy, *Pirates and Privateers* (Wayland, 1981)

Welfare, Simon and Fairley, John, *Mysterious World* (Collins, 1980)

*The Kraken, a cross between a giant squid and an octopus. Does it really exist in our oceans' depths, or only in sailors' stories?*

# Index

Africa 20
America 8, 12, 17, 22, 24, 25, 30, 32, 38, 39, 40, 44
*Architeuthis see* Kraken
Atlantic Ocean 6, 8, 10, 11, 20, 22, 23, 24, 27, 33, 40
Atlantic Ocean 6, 7
Australia 33
Azores 11, 17

Bahamas 6, 24
    Bimini 6-7
Benito, Bonito 37, 38
Bergman, Peter 38
Bermuda Triangle 8, 11, 12, 43
Blackbeard Teach 38-9
Britain 17, 27, 33, 36, 37, 40
*Brunswick* 29

Cadborosaurus ('Caddy') 33
Canada 33
Cape of Good Hope 14, 30
Caribbean 8, 10, 11, 12, 18, 38
Carthaginians 23
Cayce, Edgar 6
Central America 10, 20, 22, 37
Cocos Island 37, 38
*coelacanth* 6
Columbus, Christopher 22, 25, 44
Courtenay, James 17
Cruise-Wilkins, Reginald 35

Davies, Edmund 37
divers 6, 43
disappearing ships 8, 10-11, 12, 17, 30

Egypt 20
*Ellen Austen* 11-12
Ericson, Leif 25

First World War 8, 40
*Flying Dutchman* 14-15
Forbes, James 38

Germany 8, 19, 40
Gissler, Auguste 38
gods 42, 43
Greece 23, 35
Greenland 24, 25
*Grosvenor* 36

Henry, Capt. Don 12, 13
HMS *Daedalus* 29, 30
Heuvelmans, Dr Bernard 33
Heyerdahl, Thor 20

Iceland 25
Indian Ocean 6, 29, 35
Indonesia 14, 16, 22
Ireland 23, 40

Keating, John 38
Kidd, Capt. William 39, 46
Kraken 28, 29, 32, 47

Labrador 24
*Lady Lovibond* 17
le Vasseur, Olivier 34-5
*Lusitania* 40, 44
*Lutine* 36

manatee 43
*Marie Celeste* 17-18
*Mary Dear* 37, 38
McQuhae, Capt. 30
Mediterranean 6, 23
Meehan, Michael 17
mermaid 42
*Monongahela* 30
'Morgawr' monster 31
monsters 27, 28-33, 43

Netherlands 14, 36
Newfoundland 24, 25, 28
Norse sagas 24, 25, 28

octopus 29
*Ourang Medan* 16-17

Pacific Ocean 17, 22, 30, 37
*Pearl* 29
'Philadelphia Experiment' 11
Phoenicians 23

pirates 34-5, 37-9, 44
Proteus 43

*Quedah Merchant* 39

*Ra I* and *Ra II* 20

Saint Brendan 23-4
Sargasso Sea 10, 23
sea serpent 29, 30, 31, 32, 33
South America 22, 36
Spain 22, 37
squid 29, 43
Starkey, John 29
*Strathowen* 29
submarine 8, 19, 40

Thomson, Capt. 37
*Titanic* 45
treasure 35, 36-9, 44
    hunters 36, 38

UB65 19
UFOs 12
USS *Cyclops* 8-9, 10
USS *Pickering* 10
USS *Wasp* 10-11
USS *Wildcat* 11

van der Decken, Capt. 14
Vikings 24-5

*Waterton* 17
whales 30, 32, 43, 46
wrecks 36

## Picture acknowledgements

The publishers would like to thank the following for supplying pictures for this book: Associated Press 45 (lower); Bruce Coleman Ltd 6 (upper: G. D. Plage; lower: Carl Roessler); Mary Evans Picture Library 28, 29, 32 (lower), 42, 46; Fortean Picture Library 17, 31 (lower), 32 (upper), 33 (Robert Le Serrec), 44; PHOTRI 22 (upper), 25; Ann Ronan Picture Library 45 (upper); Ronald Sheridan 22 (lower), 43 (both). The artwork is by the following people: Tony Gibbons *cover, frontispiece,* 8-9, 10, 13, 14-15, 18, 19, 24, 36, 37, 39, 40-41; Martin Kingstone 7, 11, 16, 20-21, 23, 26-7, 31, 34-5, 38; Stephen Wheele 32.